MASKS TELL STORIES

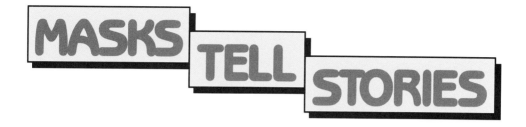

MASKS TELL STORIES

CAROL GELBER

Beyond Museum Walls
The Millbrook Press
Brookfield, Connecticut

*Cover: A mask used in Sri Lankan drama
depicts Garuda, a character in Hindu mythology.*

Library of Congress Cataloging-in-Publication Data

Gelber, Carol.
Masks tell stories / by Carol Gelber.
p.   cm.
Includes bibliographical references and index.
Summary: Describes the use of masks in ancient and
contemporary societies throughout the world, including
masks used in religious ceremonies, holiday celebrations,
theatrical performances, and daily life.
ISBN 1-56294-224-7 (lib. bdg.)
1. Masks—Social aspects—Juvenile literature.   2. Masks—
Religious aspects—Juvenile literature.   [1. Masks.]   I. Title.
GT1747.G38   1993
391'.434—dc20   92-15595   CIP   AC

Published by The Millbrook Press
2 Old New Milford Road
Brookfield, Connecticut 06804

Series Editor: Margaret Cooper

CONTENTS

INTRODUCTION

Put on a mask and you become somebody else. You feel and even act like a different person. Wear a clown mask and you will quickly find yourself trying to make people laugh. But how would you feel if you wore the mask of a wise old man? How would you act wearing a mask of a huge supernatural bird that eats human flesh?

A mask is like a poem that expresses the essence of a feeling, a spirit, or a character. Enter into that spirit as you put on a mask, and the spirit can enter into you. Whether it is a sacred mask worn in a secret ceremony or a funny face in a Halloween parade, a mask will also change the way that other people react to you.

Because masks have the power to transform our identity and affect our feelings and behavior, they play many roles in people's lives all over the world.

Perhaps the most ancient use of masks is to represent supernatural spirits. Because such masks make spirits a visible presence, they have long been used in ceremonies meant to bring people into contact with supernatural forces.

Special days like the beginning of a new year or events like a wedding are also times for mask wearing. Masks are sometimes created to honor important people. In the theater, masks enable actors to play many different characters and create eerie dramatic effects. In our daily lives, masks like a welder's helmet or a baseball catcher's mask allow us to work and play in safety.

It is convenient to separate masks into categories in order to describe them. Actually, a ceremonial mask often serves more than one purpose. A sacred mask that appears at a village funeral may be brought out again for a ceremony to bring rain or to honor an important visitor.

As we discover how different societies use masks, we find that masks can tell us stories about the people who wear them.

ONE
REACHING SPIRITS

Ice Age cave paintings, the earliest human records, show men who seem to be wearing animal masks. One famous picture engraved on a cave wall some 14,000 years ago depicts a man with the head of a bison. We can only guess at what these images mean, but it is likely that early men wore masks in ceremonies they hoped would bring them success in hunting. We know, for example, that 150 years ago the Mandan Indians of the northern American plains danced in buffalo (bison) masks, hoping to charm the buffalo spirits and bring the animals to the Indians' hunting grounds.

As far back as we can trace, people have sought ways to control the environmental forces that affect their lives, from plants and animals to the weather. Sometimes these forces are thought of as supernatural spirits that can be won over through special rituals. Masks used in these ceremonies are supposed to bring the people who wear them into contact with spirit helpers or even to transform them into spirits. A mask wearer may actually feel possessed by a spirit and speak with the spirit's voice. When ceremonial masqueraders dance, they are trying to influence the unpredictable forces that affect their lives.

GROWING UP ▪ Every society divides people into age groups with special rights and responsibilities. Babies learn to talk, children learn the rules of their society, teenagers prepare for life as adults. Often the passage from one age group to another is marked in special ways. Through events like joining a secret society or ceremonies like the Jewish bar mitzvah, boys of a certain age are recognized as men. In some societies, moving from one age group into the next is an occasion that calls for wearing masks representing ancestors or protective spirits.

Masquerading at initiation ceremonies has been a common custom in Africa, and in many places masks still appear at these ceremonies. Initiation into a secret society is often a milestone that boys must pass to be accepted as grown-up men. They may be taken away from their village to a camp in the countryside. There they undergo tests of physical strength and courage that sometimes include being marked with scars or tattoos. When they return to their village they have a new status. Childhood is over. And boys who are initiated together will have a special, lifelong bond.

The Landai Masquerader ▪ Several ethnic groups in the West African country of Liberia have a men's society known as *poro*. Years ago, all boys spent four years in *poro* camps in the countryside (called "bush schools") where they learned the traditions of their people, the art of warfare, and farming skills. Today many boys go for only the three summer months of public school vacation.

When the time comes for a group of boys to begin their initiation, clay whistles are heard from the outskirts of their village. The sound (which resembles the noise made by blowing into empty soda bottles) warns villagers that the Landai masquerader is coming to take the boys away. Women and young children are not supposed to

**Boys are led to their initiation ceremony by
the Landai masquerader of the *poro* society.**

see him, and they shut themselves in their houses. They are not allowed to go near the initiation camp.

Landai masks are very large, with huge teeth set in long crocodile jaws that are painted blood red. Old accounts say that the Landai masquerader pretended to capture the boys, chew them up, and swallow them.

The Landai appears again when the boys return from the bush school. Formerly, when the school lasted for four years, the boys would then be considered ready for adult responsibilities.

The Koko Ceremony ▪ In order to give special ceremonial names to their children, Kayapo Indians in the Brazilian rain forest hold a *koko* ceremony. Besides passing on "good names," the *koko* ceremony is also a time for celebrating the advancement of a boy into an older age group.

The ceremony begins with a procession of Kayapo men into the Indian village. They wear monkey and anteater masks that they have secretly made in the forest. Monkey masqueraders chatter in high voices and scamper about in imitation of real monkeys. People laugh at their pranks and give them small gifts of food.

The "monkeys" are young Kayapo men who are not yet fathers. Each has woven his mask from forest plants and decorated it with beads, clamshells, and tiny bells. The monkeys also wear long straw coats. No one dares to ask who they are. In the past the Kayapo would have killed anyone trying to discover a masquerader's identity.

The fiber masks of the "anteaters" cover their entire bodies. The masks are shaped like a cone with a floppy tip decorated with dangling red tassels and tinkling bells.

From time to time for three months, the anteaters come to dance in the village plaza. The *koko* ceremony ends with a feast of corn and

Kayapo "anteater" masks play an important part in the *koko* ceremony. When they first appear, the anteaters are friendly and playful. But as the weeks go by, their costumes grow shabby and they become nasty. They try to scratch the children with sharp fish teeth, sometimes making them cry.

Mariwine are ancestor spirits said to live in holes.
Their masks of baked clay are secretly made by men
and hidden in the forest, far away from the village.

tortoise pies. People tie offerings of foods onto the tips of the ant-eaters' masks. On the last day of the ceremony the anteater masks are hoisted onto long poles. Stamping their feet and thumping the poles on the ground, the men end the *koko* ceremony in a vigorous dance.

The Mariwine ▪ Masks also can be used to discipline children. They are used this way by Matis Indians who live in the South American rain forest along the northern border of Peru and Brazil. The Matis raise crops in forest clearings and hunt game with blowguns and bows and arrows. They live in smoky thatched-roof longhouses, each occupied by several families.

About once a month, just as the women and children are settled into their hammocks for the night, the Mariwine masquerader appears in a doorway of the communal house. He represents an ancestor spirit of the Matis. Squatting on his haunches, he waddles into the firelight, roaring with each step he takes. His body is coated with river mud and decorated with lacy green ferns. Two red feathers stuck in his clay mask rise above his head like long antennae. In one hand he holds a bundle of switches—one for each child.

The youngest children scream, for they know there is no escape. He will whip them, one by one, with the switches until his bundle is gone. Older children bravely present themselves for a few lashes because they believe that the Mariwine's whipping helps them grow up big and strong.

Matis parents never punish children's mischief. It is rare for mothers or fathers even to raise their voices to a child. Instead, one or two Mariwine appear shortly after the children have been unruly, and they pay special attention to children who have caused trouble in the village. Sometimes little boys make copies of the Mariwine's mask from mud and run after the little girls, threatening them with a whipping.

MASKS FOR CURING ▪ Things that cannot be explained, from lightning to a disease, may be thought to be connected with supernatural forces. Having no way to identify bacteria and viruses as the cause, some people believe that evil spirits cause illness. Getting well depends on persuading these wicked spirits to depart, often through special ceremonies. Masks used in curing ceremonies sometimes represent demons that cause the illness or good spirits that will help to cure it.

The False Face Society ▪ Curing sickness is the special purpose of the Iroquois False Face Society. Iroquois Indians have long lived in what is now the northeastern United States and Canada. For centuries they raised corn, squash, and beans and hunted animals. They built villages of longhouses, walled about with high wooden fences.

Today, many Iroquois still speak their native language, practice their ancient crafts, and take part in traditional curing ceremonies.

The False Face Society takes its name from the painted wooden masks that members wear in curing rituals. In these ceremonies, members dance to the sound of rattles made of snapping-turtle shells. To become a member, a person has to have had a special dream or been cured of illness by the False Faces.

False Face masks are carved in the trunks of living trees. This is done to capture the trees' spirit in the masks. Once cut away from the tree, the masks are painted red or black, and hairlike fiber is attached to them.

One type of mask, called "Old Broken Nose," represents a spirit who challenged the Creator of the World. To show off his power, the spirit commanded a mountain to come to him. But the mountain moved only halfway. Then the spirit turned his back and challenged the Creator of the World to move the mountain. When he turned

This False Face mask is still attached to the tree trunk from which it was carved.

around to look, the mountain was so close that he smashed his nose against it.

The Iroquois treat False Face masks with great respect. When not in use they are kept carefully stored away, face down, wrapped in clean white cloths.

Thovil Masks of Sri Lanka ▪ The island of Sri Lanka lies 25 miles (40 kilometers) off the coast of India. A legend says that when Buddha visited the island 2,500 years ago, he made a pact with local demons that plague humans with illness. These demons, the *yakas*, would have to go away if certain curing ceremonies, called Thovil, were carried out.

Many people in Sri Lanka still believe illness that modern medicine fails to cure is caused by *yakas*. For such an illness they hire a Thovil priest to perform a curing ceremony with a troupe of masked dancers. The ceremony concentrates on the most important *yakas* (there are eighteen in all), with the priest impersonating the King of the Demons.

First, the patient's horoscope is consulted for a lucky date for the ceremony. It will take place outdoors, in front of the patient's house. The entire neighborhood will be there to feast and watch the dances. Relatives and friends will have a chance to visit and comfort the patient.

A shrine is set up outside the house on the morning of the ceremony. The patient is brought out and laid on a mat. In the afternoon the Thovil priest arrives with the dancers and drummers who will perform at intervals until well into the next morning.

The dances begin solemnly, but as the night progresses they become spectacularly dramatic. The dancers twirl flaming torches and pretend to eat fire and rub it into their bodies. Late in the night

**Two sickness demons perform
in a Thovil curing ceremony.**

they put on ferocious masks and parade about calling out their demon names. Each demon explains why he is tormenting the patient.

In the morning, as the ceremony ends, the demons begin to act like ridiculous buffoons. They may, for example, run from a pet cat as though it were an angry monster. The sickness demons become laughable clowns so that the patient feels less frightened by the illness. Fears are banished with the *yakas*, and the patient is left in a healthier frame of mind.

HELPING FARMERS ▪ Everyone has to worry about illness, but for farmers the weather, especially rainfall, is another big worry. Too much or too little rain can kill crops, bringing famine and even starvation. To ensure successful harvests, farmers may perform ceremonies that include masked dances.

Hopi Kachinas ▪ In mid-December the first masked kachina dancer appears in the Hopi Indian villages in the Arizona desert. He comes into the village alone, singing in a low voice. During the next six months more and more kachina dancers will appear in the villages. They will dance to encourage the rain that brings bountiful crops, good health, and happiness to the Hopi people.

For a thousand years Hopi Indians have planted corn, beans, and squash in the dry land around their stone villages. Little rain falls on their land, but without any rain at all, crops wither and die.

"Kachina" is the name Hopis give to the spirit of all things in their world: plants, animals, natural forces like lightning and thunder, places, and Hopi ancestors. The Hopis believe that kachina spirits once lived with them in their villages. When the kachinas danced, rain fell on the land. But the Hopis didn't show them the proper respect. The kachinas left to live underground in the nearby mountains. Sometimes they can be seen floating over the mountain peaks in the form of rain clouds.

The men who wear kachina masks represent the supernatural spirits. There are more than two hundred kachinas, each with its own personality, costume, and dance. Many of them are painted with designs that stand for rain. Most kachinas are thought of as friendly to people. They act as messengers to the gods, carrying people's prayers for rain and good health.

In July kachina dancers perform the final dance of the year. The dancers give children popcorn and oranges, and small bows and arrows for the boys and kachina dolls for the girls. Then the kachina spirits return to their underground homes in the mountains.

The Chi Wara Dance ▪ As in the Arizona desert, rain is scarce in the West African savanna, home of the Bamana people of Mali. To be a good farmer in this harsh, dry land requires hard labor from sunrise to sunset. No wonder the Bamana people consider farming a job that takes a strong will as well as physical strength.

A Bamana myth tells how a spirit called Chi Wara, half animal and half human, was able to change weeds into corn and millet. He taught people how to farm. Harvests were so plentiful that people became careless. They didn't tend their fields, and they wasted grain. In anger, Chi Wara buried himself in the ground. To get his help once more, people danced in wooden headdresses made to represent him.

Chi Wara dancers are men, and they always appear in pairs. Both men wear long costumes of burlap or cotton that hide their bodies and caps topped with a wooden antelopelike sculpture. The "male" antelope has the tapering face of an anteater, an animal whose strength and endurance the Bamana prize. The "female" carries a

**Chi Wara dancers always appear in pairs.
They are selected by the elders from young
men in the village who are good farmers.**

fawn on her back. Long fiber braids sewn on the caps hang down like a veil, hiding the dancers' faces.

Both masqueraders dance bent over, leaning on sticks, a position that makes them look like four-legged animals. The male antelope is always an especially skillful dancer. He whirls and leaps in imitation of a real antelope.

Chi Wara headdresses are carved by Bamana craftsmen and decorated with pieces of red cloth and hammered metal. When not in use they are stored in the rafters over a kitchen fire. Smoke darkens the wood and protects it from wood beetles and termites.

The dance was once performed in secret by the men's Chi Wara society. As time went on, dancers performed it whenever villagers labored together in the fields. Eventually the dance was performed simply to encourage men to be good farmers. Nowadays fewer and fewer villages have a Chi Wara dance. Those that do have tourists as well as villagers in the audience.

SOCIAL HARMONY ▪ Some masked dances and ceremonies are performed to influence weather or other natural forces. But ceremonies and festivals that bring people together also reinforce their shared beliefs and traditions. These events promote cooperation and harmony among the members of a group.

The Gelede Masquerade ▪ The Yoruba people of Nigeria, a West African nation, hold elaborate masquerades known as Gelede to honor and please the spirit of Iya Nea. She is the "Great Mother of Us All," and she controls the fertility of both the land and the people. Iya Nea especially represents the power of women.

Many Yoruba towns have a Gelede association that organizes masquerades to honor the Great Mother. Members include dancers, drummers, singers, and costume makers. The dancers are always men who dance in male and "female" pairs. Dancers portraying women wear huge wooden breasts and tie banana or papaw stems around their waists to make enormous hips. Male costumes give the dancers powerful, wide shoulders. All the dancers wear iron anklets that rattle as they dance.

The carved wooden Gelede mask fits over the top part of the head. It is usually topped with a wooden sculpture that represents something in Yoruba life: a market woman's bowl of fruit, a foreigner in a funny hat, an animal, a modern sewing machine.

Gelede performances begin in the afternoon in the town's marketplace. The drummers arrive first. Men with large sticks and palm branches push at the crowd to clear a performance space. The first dancers are children, wearing bits and pieces of old costumes. Teenage dancers come next, wearing more elaborate costumes. Finally, the master dancers appear. They are able to match their steps perfectly to the beat of the drums. As excitement mounts and people surge forward to get a better view, the crowd controllers lash at their feet with palm branches to keep the space clear for the dancers. A good performance will please Iya Nea so that harvests will be successful and women will have large, healthy families.

THE ANCESTORS ▪ In her role as Great Mother, Iya Nea is a powerful ancestor spirit. Many people believe that the spirits of ancestors have powers that can help or hinder their descendants. A mask is meant to put the wearer in touch with ancestor spirits who can influence the outcome of such important events as birth, death, harvests, and warfare.

Masks From the **Tambaran House** ▪ The Iatmul people live in Papua New Guinea, part of the large island of New Guinea near Australia. No traditional Iatmul ceremony may take place without

A Yoruba Gelede masquerader wears a female
costume and a mask topped with an airplane.

Peepholes for the eyes are in the throat of this Iatmul man's costume. The mask rises well above his head, making him appear extra tall and powerful. Around his neck the masquerader wears a shaped piece of shell, a valuable possession because of its beauty and rarity.

the presence of ancestor spirits. These powerful spirits can work for good or evil, so Iatmul men's societies try to influence them with feasts and ceremonies. These societies have clubhouses called *tambaran* houses in villages along the Sepik River.

A traditional *tambaran* house is a long wooden building with a thatched roof. The huge poles that support the roof form a wide passage down the middle of the building, much like the aisle in a church. Because the Sepik River often floods, the house is built on stilts. Masks, dance costumes, and secret musical instruments like flutes and gongs belong to the *tambaran* society and are kept inside the house. Men put on masks and costumes in the privacy of the *tambaran* house. Then they come out to dance, blowing on hidden bamboo flutes whose sound is said to be the voice of ancestors.

Women and girls, and boys who are not yet members of the men's society, are strictly forbidden to enter the *tambaran* house. In the past, trespassing would have been punished by death. In those times, violent raids on neighboring villages were common. Fights were frequent, partly because Sepik River people claimed ownership of everything they valued. All useful plants belonged to someone. Even some wild birds had "owners." All these possessions were jealously defended. Sometimes, when discipline was needed, a masked ancestor spirit prowled the village, striking terror with the whine of his hidden flute. His presence warned troublemakers to expect supernatural punishment if they continued to misbehave.

African Ancestor Masks ▪ The Songye people of central Africa also called on ancestor spirits to help maintain law and order.

The Songye once ruled a vast region in what is now the nation of Zaire. Threats of magical punishment helped their rulers maintain power. The rulers controlled the men's mask societies and used them as a kind of police force. Masqueraders representing ancestor spirits intimidated people with threats that evil magic would be used against them if they broke the rules of their society. Today mask associations are still active in some isolated Songye villages.

Ancestor spirits are also important to the Dogon people, who live in a beautiful but rugged and isolated part of the African country of Mali. Because of their isolation, the Dogon have preserved many of their traditional ceremonies and dances. Today, however, they perform their masked dances for tourists as well.

Masked dances take place at funerals and at Dama ceremonies held every two or three years. Spirits of the dead are believed to wander around their old homes. Funeral and Dama ceremonies lead these spirits into the realm of Dogon ancestors. When a very important person dies, a special "Great Dama" may be held, with as many as four hundred masked dancers.

The more than seventy-five types of Dogon masks belong to men's mask societies called *awa*. Each village *awa* makes different kinds of masks. Best known is the painted *kanaga* mask, topped with a tall structure of wooden bars. In the Dama ceremony, *kanaga* masks are worn by groups of dancers who leap into the air and then bend to touch the tips of their masks to the ground. If the performance is especially good, old Dogon men in the audience tap the ground with their walking sticks.

Every sixty years the Dogon hold a ceremony that celebrates the beginning of a new generation. At this time each village carves a new "great mask." It represents the mythical snake into which the first Dogon ancestor to die was transformed. The great mask can be up to thirty-six feet tall, much too large to be worn. It is kept hidden in a rock shelter near the village. At funerals it is carried to the house of the dead person as a mark of respect.

A Songye masquerader wearing a female mask (male masks have crests). Only certain men are allowed to wear these masks. Mask carvers are skilled craftsmen who work alone and in secret.

Dogon dance masks represent ancestors that may be humans or animals. The *kanaga* mask is said to represent a bird.

Nowadays people everywhere have television sets and radios and feel connected to modern ways of life. Small societies are less isolated. Their beliefs and ceremonies are changing as they have more contact with other parts of the world. In some places, new ideas blend with old traditions. In other areas, the old traditions are lost. There are fewer places in the world today where people use masks for reaching spirits.

TWO
CELEBRATING SPECIAL DAYS

Masked carnivals may welcome the first day of spring, the beginning of a new year, or a day honoring a particular god or saint. Sometimes masks help tell the story of a historical event. And an important personal event like a wedding is a time to wear a veil, a special kind of mask with a long tradition.

Masks are often used in ceremonies or celebrations that occur only at special times of the year. Sometimes the masks that appear at these events originated solely to add to the festivities. On other occasions, the masks may come from old traditions that have changed or lost their original meaning. And some special days are celebrated with ceremonial masquerades that are part of a sacred ritual.

HALLOWEEN ▪ Halloween masks and trick-or-treating come from very old European traditions. In ancient Ireland and Scotland, the date our calendar calls October 31 was considered the end of summer and the last day of the year. The Celtic peoples of those places believed that it was a day when goblins and witches roamed the countryside and ghosts returned to visit their families. In the evening, villagers lit huge bonfires on hilltops, perhaps to frighten off witches.

Then, in the Middle Ages, Christianity spread through the British Isles. The Church wanted to put an end to pagan Celtic customs. Christians were urged to observe October 31 as All Hallows' Eve, the evening before All Saints' Day. But old beliefs were hard to stamp out. In country villages, people continued to light bonfires, and boys and girls in masks and costumes played pranks on their neighbors. Like mischievous goblins, they hid farmers' tools and turned barnyard animals loose. In Ireland, groups of merrymakers went from house to house demanding food and drink.

In the nineteenth century large numbers of Irish emigrated to the United States. By the end of the 1800s many of their Halloween customs had become part of the American holiday. Today it is largely schoolchildren who masquerade at Halloween, collecting "trick or treat" candy from their neighbors. Some masks are homemade, but most come from stores. Witches, ghosts, and clowns are old favorites.

There are times when Halloween pranks turn into destructive vandalism. To discourage this behavior, many cities promote other ways to celebrate the holiday. New York City's Halloween costume parade, for example, has become one of its most entertaining events.

THE TIBETAN NEW YEAR ▪ The Celtic people of ancient Europe linked the new year to harvest time. Many other peoples celebrate New Year's Day after the shortest hours of daylight in the sun's yearly cycle. Some, including the people of Tibet, use the moon's cycles to fix the date.

**Father and daughter monsters enjoy
New York City's Halloween parade.**

In their ferocious masks, these Tibetan monks represent supernatural defenders of the Buddhist faith.

Tibet lies on the world's highest plateau, surrounded by the forbidding Himalayan Mountains. It is no wonder that the country was little known to outsiders until the twentieth century. There were few roads, and Tibet did not make foreigners welcome. For hundreds of years Tibet was isolated, developing a unique branch of the Buddhist religion with distinctive customs and ceremonies.

Today Tibet is occupied by the Chinese, who have suppressed traditional religious practices. But Tibetan traditions continue in Tibetan settlements in India and Nepal.

Tibetans observe their new year (which falls in our February or March) with festivities that last several weeks. Ceremonies actually begin before New Year's Day. Everyone wants the year to begin without misfortune. Ordinary people give their house a fresh coat of whitewash and decorate it with good luck symbols made of cloth or paper. Buddhist monks perform rituals and masked *cham* dances to drive away demons and evil spirits.

Cham dances take place outdoors, watched by crowds of Tibetans. One of the dances performed at this time is the dance of Chojeh, the Lord of the Dead. He wears a bull-like green mask with bulging eyes, and five yellow skulls form a row between his horns. Chojeh is accompanied by many other dancers in ferocious masks with horns and skulls. As the dancers whirl and hop around the dancing ground, Chojeh's escorts move through the crowd collecting gifts of thread, walnuts, needles, and small coins. These gifts are payment for the monks' prayers for the dead.

On the night before New Year's Day parents lay out new clothes for their sleeping children. The year should be greeted in one's very best clothes. On New Year's Day men wearing masks made of cotton go from house to house offering greetings that are meant to bring good luck in the coming year. Householders offer them food and small amounts of money.

CARNIVAL ▪ Since medieval times there have been carnivals in Roman Catholic countries before the season known as Lent. Early Christians observed the forty-day period of Lent with prayer and fasting. There were strict bans on rich foods like butter and meat. (In fact, the word *carnival* comes from Latin words meaning "farewell to meat.")

Before they had to give up their favorite foods, people customarily held parties, feasts, and masked carnivals. It is likely that these pre-Lent carnivals took the place of ancient Roman festivals. The origin of carnival masks is uncertain, but in many places in Europe masks were once worn during festival times. Disguised by a mask, revelers could act in ways that were ordinarily forbidden.

Lent always begins on Ash Wednesday, a day Catholics still observe with special church services. In times when modern methods of food storage were unknown, foods prohibited during Lent had to be eaten before Ash Wednesday or they would be wasted. Tuesday, then, became a day to stuff oneself with fattening foods that would be forbidden for the next forty days. The French called the day *Mardi Gras*, which means "fat Tuesday."

French settlers brought Mardi Gras customs to the American city of New Orleans. The city's carnival is now world-famous. Each year thousands of tourists jam the streets of New Orleans to watch the Mardi Gras parades of colorful floats and masqueraders.

MEXICAN *TIGRE* DANCE ▪ Important historical events like famous battles or conquests can also be celebrated with masquerades. Mexican villages often celebrate national and religious holidays with fiestas, celebrations that include masked dances in the village plaza.

One dance often performed in Mexican village festivals is the *tigre* dance. *Tigre* is the Spanish word for the jaguar, the largest cat in the Americas.

A gold sunburst mask highlights this swashbuckling Mardi Gras costume.

The pre-Columbian people of Mexico called the jaguar "king of beasts." Because of its courage and ferocity, Aztec warriors considered it their guardian spirit. Only rulers could wear its cinnamon-colored skin, marked with black spots that symbolized the starry night sky. The jaguar's image was painted, modeled in clay, and carved in stone by ancient Mexican artists.

Today, although few of them will ever see one except in a zoo, Mexicans still admire the jaguar. *Tigre* is one of the most popular masks made in modern Mexico. The mask makers may have never seen the real animal, so they use their imagination to create ferocious-looking *tigres* with fangs, bristly whiskers, and huge eyes.

In the many versions of the *tigre* dance, there may be one or more *tigres* who carry long whips to snap at the audience. In one dance, boys wearing masks of farm animals like goats and donkeys are caught and carried off by the whip-cracking *tigres*. The *tigres* may even run into the crowd, chasing and frightening small children. A "doctor" pretends to bandage the "wounded." At last, a masquerader costumed as a dog called Maravilla appears to track down the *tigres*. With Maravilla's help, men with toy shotguns kill the *tigres* and drag them away.

Tigre masks were used in ancient Mexican ceremonies. Today, although they remain an important part of fiesta entertainment, *tigres* have lost their original significance. Nevertheless, old beliefs persist. For example, a certain ancient *tigre* mask is said to be kept in a chest in the Mexican city of Guerrero. When the chest is opened, the *tigre* supposedly moves its eyes, blinks, and stares at the person who stands over it.

HIDING THE BRIDE ▪ We don't usually think of personal celebrations as occasions for wearing masks, but weddings can be an exception.

Tigre masqueraders wear yellow costumes
with black spots and masks that come straight
from the imagination of the mask maker.

In this Hindu wedding of two wealthy, upper-class Indians, the bride remains completely veiled. The bride and groom sit before the sacred fire, which they will circle during the ceremony. The groom holds objects that are believed to bring the couple good luck.

Here comes the bride—but you can't see her face. In a formal church wedding the bride comes down the aisle with her face hidden beneath a lacy white veil. Wearing a bridal veil is a relatively new wedding tradition in the United States, but the custom of masking a bride's face has a long history.

A bride's veil was originally intended to disguise and protect her from the dangers that lurked about the wedding ceremony. Marriage, one of the most important events in anyone's life, is always accompanied by powerful emotions and concern for the future. Many people believe that dangerous forces—like bad luck—must be kept away from the marriage ceremony. Our own tradition that a lucky bride must wear "something old, something new, something borrowed, something blue" is an example of these beliefs.

Wealthy Chinese brides once traveled to their new households in beautifully decorated sedan chairs that completely hid them from public view. In the North African country of Morocco, a bride would be carried on muleback to her future husband's house. She was not only veiled but completely enclosed in a box made of flowering branches. So concealed, the bride was protected from envious or evil eyes that might do her harm. Many Moroccan brides are still heavily veiled.

At wedding ceremonies in ancient India, an archer shot arrows into the air saying, "I pierce the eye of the demons which are sneaking around this bride." Even today it is the custom for Hindu brides to be completely veiled during the wedding ceremony, which takes several days to perform.

In some societies a wife is secluded within her husband's household, and she must wear a face-covering veil in any public place. Aside from her husband, the only men allowed to see her face are certain close relatives. The wedding veil also suggests this custom of limiting women's ability to move freely in society.

THREE
THEATER MASKS

A beautiful young woman, a frightful demon, a wild animal: with a mask an actor can instantly become any of these characters because the audience immediately believes in his new identity. A mask may even help a performer to feel and act like a different character.

We can trace back the use of masks in the theater to very early civilizations. In both ancient Greece and Japan, masks were used in religious ceremonies. In time some of these ceremonies gradually lost their religious meaning and became pure entertainment.

Today masks are still worn by performers all over the world. Some types of masks come from traditions handed down over many centuries. Even the masks themselves may be hundreds of years old. But masks are also used in new ways. Many modern theater companies continue to rely on masks to help them tell stories.

GREEK THEATER MASKS ▪ The earliest theater masks that we know of were worn by actors in the sixth century B.C., in ancient Greece. Every spring the citizens of Athens took a holiday to honor Dionysus, the Greek god of plants and wine. They celebrated with concerts, games, contests in poetry and chorus singing, and three whole days of play-going.

Plays were performed outdoors in a hillside arena, more like a modern sports stadium than what we think of as a theater. Performances began early in the morning and lasted all day. No more than three actors, always men, played all the roles. The stories they enacted were explained and commented on by a large chorus of masked singers and musicians.

Playwrights trained the actors and musicians and also designed the costumes and masks. One of the first playwrights we know about was a poet named Thespis. (Some people today still call actors "thespians.") The ancient Greeks claimed that Thespis was the first to use masks in the theater. His masks were made from canvaslike fabric, painted white for female characters and a dark color for males.

Later Greek theater masks covered the head completely, exaggerating its size. Eyeballs were painted white, with pupils left open as peepholes. Mouths were open squares or trumpet-shaped. The mask rested on the wide, padded shoulders of the actor's costume. Padding, platform-soled shoes, and a mask made an actor appear larger than life-size. Increasing his size with a mask and costume and his voice with a trumpet-shaped mouth helped the audience to see and hear the play.

Masks also allowed a few actors to portray many different characters. In the second century A.D. a playwright listed twenty-eight masks necessary to play all the roles in a Greek tragic drama. Another writer made a list of forty-four masks used in comedy.

Because they were made from perishable materials like linen and cork, no early Greek masks have survived. We know how they looked from ancient sculptures and paintings that show actors wearing them.

JAPANESE NOH MASKS ▪ The old masks and traditions of ancient Greek theater disappeared long ago, but traditional masked theater continues in Japan.

In plays written centuries ago for the six-hundred-year-old Japanese Noh theater, actors wearing splendid costumes and eerie wooden masks glide slowly onto the stage. They chant their stories, accompanied by a chorus of voices, a flute, and drums. The actors' gestures barely suggest the emotions they express. To express sorrow, an actor flutters a fan before his mask. To show overwhelming happiness he may tilt his mask upward. The play seems to unfold in slow motion.

The actors speak an old-fashioned form of Japanese. Members of the audience, who sit facing an almost bare stage, often bring copies of a play to the theater so that they can follow the story. A few simply shaped pieces of wood or bamboo indicate a temple, a boat, or whatever setting is needed. Masks, costumes, music, dance, and words combine to form a beautiful work of art.

The same types of Noh masks have been copied and recopied over many generations. Some masks in use today were made by famous mask carvers hundreds of years ago. Many of these masterpieces have been declared national treasures by the government of Japan.

Like the actors' gestures, Noh masks are highly refined. They are meant to show the underlying nature of human and supernatural characters. Almost three hundred different masks are needed to portray all the men, women, gods, and demons in the Noh plays. Many of them, especially masks of young men and women, are expressionless. The way the actor tilts his head, the lighting, and the imagination of the audience make the mask seem happy or sad.

Traditionally, the Noh actors are men. Before a performance, the

**With the help of masks, men
play all the roles in Noh theater.**

leading actor carefully considers which mask he will wear. His choice will determine the costume he selects and the kind of performance he will give. Before his assistant ties the mask to his face, the actor holds the mask in front of him and greets it as a sign of respect. It is said that a good Noh actor does not put on a mask, but that the mask pulls his face into it.

Years ago, women were not even supposed to touch a Noh mask. But today a well-known Noh mask maker, Akiko Taniguchi, is a woman. She works in a small straw-matted studio in Tokyo. It takes her forty days to finish a mask, using half the time for the carving. She then coats the front of the mask with fine white clay, sands it down, and paints it. Art collectors are eager to buy her masks, but she prefers to sell them to actors who will bring them to life on the stage.

KWAKIUTL DANCE-DRAMAS • In the elaborate ceremonial dance-dramas of the Kwakiutl Indians we can see how masked theater begins. The Kwakiutl live on Canada's Vancouver Island and along the nearby Pacific coast. They once depended on fish from the ocean and the rivers that run out of the dark forests above their villages. In the summer they lived in temporary camps, fishing for the red salmon they loved. The rainy winters were a time for ceremonies and entertainment that featured masked dances.

In the past Kwakiutl masked dances were performed in a firelit communal house. The performers had many theatrical tricks. Spirits came flying down the smoke hole of the house, heads were cut off and attached again, voices came from empty corners of the room. An octopus mask with long wooden tentacles could seem to swim across the room. In the flickering firelight, the huge painted masks must have been thrillingly dramatic.

Kwakiutl dancers pose for a photograph in 1915.

There is a great variety of Kwakiutl masks, many representing animals. Some can be snapped open by the performer to reveal a second mask inside the first, transforming the head of a whale to a human face, for example. Some masks represent savage spirits who are dangerous to humans. One such bloodthirsty creature is a skull-cracking bird whose enormous beak can open and close. Another is a cannibal woman named Dzunukwa, who behaves very much like a wicked witch in a fairy tale. Each kind of mask helps dancers tell a story from the past.

Masks, and the songs and dances that go with them, are owned by families. To this day these rights remain an important form of family property. As with other kinds of wealth, owning them gives a family high standing in the community.

RANGDA AND THE BARONG • On the island of Bali, near the equator and across the Pacific Ocean from the Kwakiutl homeland, masked dances also are performed as both ceremony and drama.

On a map of the world, the island of Bali is a tiny speck in the Pacific. Yet this little Indonesian island has an influence far beyond its size. It is famous for its tropical beauty and its arts. Every village has organizations devoted to dance, music, and the dramatic performance of stories connected to Bali's Hindu religion.

Masks and costumes for one of the best-known Balinese dances are stored in every village temple. The dance concerns the eternal battle between Rangda, a terrifying witch, and the Barong, a fierce but benevolent protective spirit. The Barong and Rangda represent opposites: day and night, right and left, good and evil.

Rangda wears a costume of feathers and a grotesque mask with fangs, a long snakelike tongue, and bulging eyes. The evils she brings include such human disasters as disease and death. Her vile deeds include robbing graves and casting spells over people.

This Balinese dancer represents Rangda, the evil witch who can never be destroyed.

The Barong, a lion that looks more like a dragon, also has a ferocious mask, with protruding eyes and long teeth. But he is a good spirit. His face appears everywhere on doors and gateways to prevent evil from entering temples and houses. The dragonlike Barong is always played by two men under a cloth, one in front working the mask and the other behind, representing the Barong's hind legs.

The performance of the Rangda-Barong dance is a wonderfully entertaining spectacle. The dance represents the eternal struggle of good and evil. The Barong is never killed. Rangda is never destroyed. But the dance proclaims that whenever evil appears, the Barong will be there to help overcome it.

FOLK THEATER IN KOREA ▪ Masked dances from the countryside of Korea, opposite Japan on the east coast of Asia, tell a different kind of story. Centuries ago masked dancers performed in the palaces of Korean rulers, to entertain their important foreign visitors. Performers were paid to appear regularly at court events until the seventeenth century. Then the government stopped paying them, and the dancers began to travel around the Korean countryside, giving performances for farmers and villagers.

It is said that some two hundred years ago a troupe of actors didn't show up for a performance in the town of Yangju. The disappointed townspeople decided they would put on an entertainment of their own. They made their own masks and gave a performance that was such a success that Yangju citizens have performed masked dance-drama, called Yangju *pyolsandae*, ever since. With masked dance, mime, and song, *pyolsandae* tells old stories that poke fun at uppity aristocrats, corrupt officials, and quarreling husbands and wives. Performances, which can be all-day affairs, take place on major holidays and at events such as village weddings and important birthdays.

A comic *pyolsandae* performer tries to teach a baby doll the Korean alphabet.

The twenty-two masks used in Yangju *pyolsandae* are made from dried gourds. Holes for the eyes and mouth are carved out, and a nose and eyebrows are glued on. Several layers of paper are pasted over the mask, which is then painted in brilliant colors. One type of mask has brass eyelids that can open and close.

By 1950 performances of Yangju *pyolsandae* had almost disappeared. Recently, however, young Koreans have become interested in preserving their country's folk arts, and many Korean schools now have groups who present these traditional dance-dramas.

NEW MASKS, OLD TALES ▪ While masks are used most commonly in traditional theater like the Japanese Noh and Korean *pyolsandae*, actors in modern theater continue to find new ways to use them.

Every summer masked actors of the Mettawee River Company present plays on New England's village greens, in parks, and in fields. The stories acted out are based on folklore, myths, and old fairy tales. The company hopes to show that these stories have themes that are universal to all societies.

The actors have to learn how to speak and move to bring the masks to life. The company's director, Ralph Lee, says that actors must learn to put their own personalities in the passenger seat and let the mask do the driving.

In his New York City studio, Lee makes the company's masks as well as masks for operas, ballets, stage plays, and television shows. He says that his career had its beginning in stories he and his brother made up about their toy animals when they were children. His very first masks were made to wear in a Halloween parade.

FOUR
MASKS FOR IMPORTANT PEOPLE

People in many societies make masks that honor important persons. Some of these masks are meant to transform a dead leader into a god or into a protective spirit who lives on in the supernatural world. Some are intended to help guide a person in the journey to the afterworld.

Other masks are simply portraits, made to honor a person of authority and prominence or to satisfy public curiosity about such a person's appearance.

KING TUTANKHAMEN ▪ King Tutankhamen's tomb lay undisturbed in Egypt's Valley of the Kings for more than three thousand years. Then, in 1922, a British archaeologist named Howard Carter discovered the underground staircase that led to the sealed doorway of Tutankhamen's burial chambers. When he was finally able to pry out some stones and peer into the tomb by candlelight, his excited companion asked, "Can you see anything?" "Yes, wonderful things!" replied Carter, for he was looking at figures of strange animals, treasure boxes, statues, and "gold—everywhere the glint of gold."

Tutankhamen's headdress is decorated with the head of a cobra (the symbol of Lower Egypt) and a vulture (the symbol of Upper Egypt) to show that Tutankhamen is ruler of all of Egypt.

Mummies of ancient Egyptian kings had been found before, but all the tombs where they lay had been robbed of the treasures buried with them. However, not only Tutankhamen's mummy but most of his tomb furnishings and his personal possessions had survived. One of the most astonishing objects in the tomb was the mask that covered the mummy's head and shoulders. Three thousand years later, it remains one of the most dazzling works of artistry ever created.

Made of solid gold, the mask is probably a good likeness of the young ruler, who died when he was about eighteen years old. The mask is inlaid with semiprecious stones, colored glass, and lapis lazuli, a mineral valued for its lovely blue color. Imitating the fashion of the time, the mask's eyes are outlined in lapis lazuli, and the ears are pierced for earrings. (The earrings have never been found.) Protective magic spells are engraved on the back and shoulders of the mask.

Tutankhamen's mummy was intended as a home for his soul, which would be transformed into a supernatural being. The golden mask also identifies Tutankhamen with the sun god, Ra, whose body was made of gold.

CHIMU BURIAL MASKS ▪ The ancient Egyptians weren't the only people who buried their god-kings with splendid treasure and masks of gold. Centuries before Columbus, in what is now the South American country of Peru, the Chimu people bundled their dead kings in many layers of finely woven cloth to which a golden mask was attached. The mask was made of thinly hammered gold, sometimes decorated with red paint or mosaics made of brightly colored feathers. The masked mummy bundle was placed in a tomb filled with the king's most prized possessions.

Today the ruins of the Chimu city of Chanchan cover several miles of Peru's northern coast. Inside the crumbling walls of its huge compounds there were once streets, houses, irrigated gardens, temples, and royal cemeteries.

Spanish conquerors invaded Peru in 1532 and were amazed at the amount of gold they found in Chanchan. They literally mined the royal tombs for gold and stripped Chimu temples of their gold and silver decoration. Priceless Chimu treasures were melted into gold and silver bars and shipped back to Spain. The gold recovered from just one Chanchan temple was worth over one million Spanish pesos.

So much treasure was buried in Chanchan tombs that the ruins of the city today are pitted with holes made by five centuries of grave robbers.

DOGS WITH HUMAN FACES ▪ In the last century, grave robbers looking for gold also ransacked many ancient tombs in western Mexico. It was a useless quest, since metalworking was unknown in Mexico almost two thousand years ago when the tombs were made. The robbers did find hundreds of polished pottery figurines of plants, animals, and humans. They thought so little of these charming pottery figures that they sometimes used them as targets for shooting practice.

Now many figures like these, discovered by later archaeologists, can be seen in museums. Especially delightful are little potbellied dogs that resemble modern Chihuahuas. Many of these dogs wear human masks, some of them only big enough to cover the dog's nose.

The Aztecs, who lived much later in central Mexico, had a dog-god whose job it was to guide souls in the afterworld. Very likely, these mask-wearing pottery dogs were meant to be faithful companions and guides for the souls of the dead.

Traces of cinnabar, a red pigment, can still be seen on this golden Chimu burial mask. Chimu kings and nobles wore nose ornaments and enormous earrings.

Pottery dogs with human masks sometimes were placed in tombs of important people in western Mexico more than a thousand years ago.

KINGS AND PRESIDENTS ▪ The mummy masks of ancient Egypt and Peru were meant to help transform their kings into rulers in an afterlife. Sometimes, however, masks served as substitutes for a dead king.

In the fifteenth century, when a French king died, an artist was called to the palace to make a wax mask of his face. The mask, complete with real hair and beard, was attached to a life-size puppet dressed in the king's coronation robes. This figure was placed on a "bed of honor" in a great reception room where nobles and courtiers came to pay their last respects to the dead king. Later the figure was displayed in a funeral procession that wound through the streets of Paris.

Masks such as the French king's served an important purpose. Before the invention of photography, masks as well as portraits showed the curious public what famous people looked like.

Our first president, George Washington, was one of the most famous men of his time. Many artists came to his home in Mount Vernon eager to paint his portrait or make a "life mask" in plaster. Washington detested having people stare at him. Sitting for a portrait was bad enough, but having a life mask made was downright embarrassing. About one such experience he wrote:

> He oiled my features over, and, placing me flat upon my back upon a cot, proceeded to daub my face with the plaster. Whilst in this ludicrous attitude, Mrs. Washington entered the room, and seeing my face thus overspread with plaster, involuntarily exclaimed. Her cry excited in me a disposition to smile. . . .

Washington goes on to confess that his smile was responsible for the unnatural twist of his lips in the sculptor's finished work.

President George Washington felt badgered by artists who wanted to make plaster life masks of his face.

We no longer rely on life masks or artists' portraits to know what our leaders look like—we see them every night on the television screen. That doesn't mean that we have no use for masks of leaders, however. Today such masks are apt to be funny faces worn at masquerade parties, for amusement, or at political protests, to ridicule the leaders they represent.

FIVE

MASKS IN DAILY LIFE

Masks used in daily life generally offer some kind of protection. A surgeon's mask, a welder's helmet, a diver's mask—all permit people to work in dangerous surroundings. Special protective masks are standard gear for many kinds of sports. Armored masks once protected knights from arrows and spears, while soldiers today may carry masks to protect them from poison gas.

SAMURAI MASKS ▪ "Devils enough to frighten anyone!" said an ancient Korean admiral about the Japanese samurai warriors he met in their iron helmets and terrifying masks. Indeed, samurai masks provided more than mere protection—they were designed to frighten the enemy. Masks had ferocious expressions, sometimes finished off with bristly eyebrows and a mustache of horsehair. Helmets were studded with iron rivets and decorated with menacing horns. Body armor of metal plates completed the samurai's costume.

For more than seven hundred years the samurai were a hereditary group of military men in Japan. They lived by a strict code of behavior that called for stern self-control and absolute loyalty to the warlord they served.

The samurai were at their height in the sixteenth century, an age of war in Japan. Rival warlords fought for control of the country with armies led by samurai warriors. On the battlefield, the color of his armor and the form of his helmet and mask identified each warrior and proclaimed the glory of his family and his lord.

BEAR FIGHTER ▪ No one would want to attract the attention of a wild bear without some kind of protection. A full-grown bear is a dangerous animal to hunt, especially if the hunter has no gun. Yet Siberian hunters in Russia did, apparently, hunt for bears armed only with a spear and hunting knives. Certainly, anyone who faced a bear in close combat needed protective armor from head to toe.

Travel books from the mid-nineteenth century describe armor-clad hunters who fought and killed bears with long-bladed knives. Even older pictures from the sixteenth century show bear hunters wearing suits of armor. One thing is sure—an armored hunter couldn't climb a tree or run away. He'd have to stand his ground and fight.

HOCKEY MASKS ▪ Ice hockey can be a dangerous sport. It has been called the fastest game on earth. The hard rubber hockey puck flies across the ice with what seems to be the force and speed of a bullet. "My business is getting shot at," Jacques Plante used to say. He was the goaltender for the Montreal Canadiens in 1959, when he became the first professional player to wear a protective mask.

Plante had good reasons for wanting a mask. In his years as a professional goalie, his nose was broken four times, and he received almost two hundred stitches to sew up cuts on his head.

The flame and gold color of this armor identified the wearer as a member of a princely family.

The bear-hunting costume of leather with metal spikes was made in the nineteenth century. Supposedly, bears feared the porcupinelike spikes and were reluctant to attack a person wearing them.

**The goalie for the Washington Capitals
wears a patriotic red, white, and blue mask
with a picture of the Capitol dome.**

The first hockey masks made goalies look like creatures from outer space. They were flesh-colored form-fitting faces of fiberglass, with thin strips of sponge rubber inside to cushion the impact of the puck. Gerry Cheevers, a goalie for the Boston Bruins, decorated his mask with stitch marks. After every game he would examine the places his mask had been hit by the puck. "Well," he would say, "that hit was worth about eight stitches," and he would draw that many stitches on his mask with a felt-tip pen. Eventually the entire mask was covered with little stitch marks.

Now all professional hockey players are required to wear protective helmets, and many of them add a clear Plexiglas face shield. Goalies' masks are no longer form-fitting faces but more like helmets with protective face cages, like a baseball catcher's mask. They are decorated with their team's emblem or colors. The chin of the Calgary Flames' goalie mask is painted with red and yellow flames that seem to lap about his ears. Little white horns decorate the red and green mask of the New Jersey Devils. A New York Buffalo Sabres goalie wears—yes, an American buffalo on his forehead.

HOSPITAL MASKS ▪ Most protective masks shield us from dangers we can see. But masks can also save us from invisible threats.

Before they knew that bacteria cause infection, doctors in Europe believed that bad air, evil odors—and even bad weather—were the cause. Doctors tended their patients with dirty hands, and bandages were apt to be torn strips of old, unwashed clothing. Hospitals were ill-kept, deadly places where half the patients died of bacterial infections.

Then, in the mid-1800s, a young English surgeon, Joseph Lister, read about some experiments that had been carried out in France by Louis Pasteur. Pasteur had proved that bacteria in the air could cause wine to spoil, and he showed that heat could kill the bacteria. Lister immediately grasped how this idea might apply to human infections. He tried painting patients' wounds with an antiseptic called carbolic acid, and he had it sprayed in the air of his operating room. Surgical patients who would have died previously began to survive.

Soon it became clear that some bacteria often present in people's throats and noses caused the most serious infections. Around the turn of the century, surgeons began to wear masks as well as special operating-room gowns and rubber gloves. Nurses and visitors in wards for infectious diseases were also required to wear masks.

The first masks were made of cotton cloth that could be washed and reused. Now, like surgical caps, gowns, and gloves, they are made of disposable material. For certain operations in which infection would be very damaging, surgeons nowadays are completely hooded by a mask connected to an air hose.

SWIM MASKS ▪ Masks have also made it possible for humans to explore the undersea world. The famous French diver Jacques Cousteau helped invent scuba diving equipment in 1943. Before that time, only a handful of professional divers managed to investigate the ocean bottom. They had to wear a heavy diving suit and a metal helmet with a glass window, connected to a surface air hose. Lead-lined boots helped them to walk on the ocean floor. Diving gear was clumsy and very expensive.

The modern diver's mask is made of silicon, with eye goggles of tempered glass. It protects the eyes and allows the diver to see clearly underwater. The mask fits tightly against the nose and mouth to help keep the diver from inhaling water. A tube connects the mouth to an airtank on the diver's back. With modern scuba equipment, a diver can stay underwater for up to an hour and move about as freely as a fish.

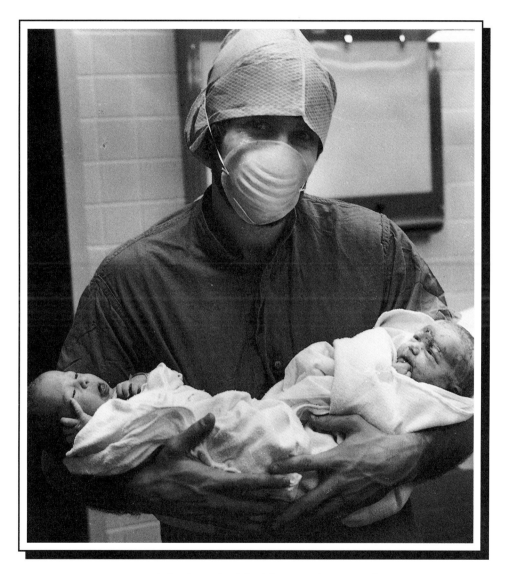

**A proud father holds his newborn twins.
His hospital mask protects the babies from being
infected by any germs their father may carry.**

There are still professional divers who wear heavy diving suits and helmets that enable them to stay underwater for a long time. Among other things, they make their living salvaging sunken ships or collecting sponges on the ocean floor. Other professionals, like some marine biologists and aquarium workers, need the freedom that scuba equipment gives them.

Many more people dive for sport than for work. In fact, an estimated three million people in the world now dive, most of them simply for the pleasure of exploring a rarely seen world—through a window provided by a mask.

FURTHER READING

Baylor, Byrd. *They Put On Masks*. Scribner, 1974.

Horner, Deborah. *Masks of the World to Cut Out and Wear*. Scribner, 1977.

Hunt, Kari, and B. W. Carlson. *Masks and Mask Makers*. Abingdon Press, 1961.

Laliberte, Norman. *Masks, Face Coverings, and Headgear*. Van Nostrand Reinhold, 1973.

Lommel, Andreas. *Masks*. McGraw-Hill, 1972.

Naylor, Penelope. *Black Images*. Doubleday, 1973.

Price, Christine. *Dancing Masks of Africa*. Scribner, 1975.

————. *The Mystery of Masks*. Scribner, 1978.

Terry, Ellen, and Lynne Anderson. *Makeup & Masks*. Rosen Group, 1982.

INDEX

ABOUT THE AUTHOR

Carol Gelber has written extensively for
Faces, *the children's anthropology magazine,*
and other publications

After earning a bachelor's degree with honors
in anthropology at Hunter College, she worked
for eight years in various capacities at the
anthropology department of the American Museum
of Natural History in New York City.

That work, which included fieldwork in Nigeria,
gave rise to her fascination with masks.

She lives in New York with her husband,
playwright Jack Gelber.

AR BL
7.6